CHINESE RECIPES

The Ultimate Classic Recipes Quick and Easy Dishes to Prepare at Home

(Delicious Chinese Recipes at Your Fingertips)

Boyd Crawford

Published by Sharon Lohan

© Boyd Crawford

All Rights Reserved

Chinese Recipes: The Ultimate Classic Recipes Quick and Easy Dishes to Prepare at Home (Delicious Chinese Recipes at Your Fingertips)

ISBN 978-1-990334-31-3

All rights reserved. No part of this guide may be reproduced in any form without permission in writing from the publisher except in the case of brief quotations embodied in critical articles or reviews.

Legal & Disclaimer

The information contained in this book is not designed to replace or take the place of any form of medicine or professional medical advice. The information in this book has been provided for educational and entertainment purposes only.

The information contained in this book has been compiled from sources deemed reliable, and it is accurate to the best of the Author's knowledge; however, the Author cannot guarantee its accuracy and validity and cannot be held liable for any errors or omissions. Changes are periodically made to this book. You must consult your doctor or get professional medical advice before using any of the suggested remedies, techniques, or information in this book.

Table of contents

Part 1 1
Introduction 2
Stir Fry Sichuan Style Prawns 4
Chicken Chow Mein 6
Beef with Oyster Sauce 8
Cashew Chicken 10
Chinese Pork Balls 12
Chinese Five Spice Chicken Thighs 14
Fried Rice with Prawn 16
Stir Fried Greens 18
Tofu & Hazelnut with Noodles 20
Egg Fried Rice 22
Ginger & Garlic Pork 24
Sweet & Sour Chicken 25
Kale with Oyster sauce 28
Chinese Steamed Bass 29
Crispy Chinese pork 31
Baked Chinese Wings 33
Chinese Style Chilli Beef 35
Shrimp with Slaw 37
Crispy Wontons 39

- Chinese Egg Soup 41
- Beef & Broccoli 43
- Sweet & Sour Pork 45
- Kung Pao Chicken 48
- Orange Chicken 50
- Pineapple Fried Rice 52
- Chinese Pepper Steaks 54
- Baked Chicken Wings with Hoisin Sauce 56
- Chicken with Bok Choy 57
- Stir Fried Shrimp & Broccoli 59
- Vegetables, Fried Rice 61
- Sesame Noodles 63
- Chinese Chicken Salad 65
- Stir Fry Sugar Snap Peas 67
- Salmon with Gingery Green Beans 69
- Honey Prawns 71
- Chinese Grilled Chicken 73
- Corn Soup 75
- Hot & Sour Soup 77
- Chinese Roasted Ribs 79
- Sautéed Green Beans 81
- Salt & Pepper Tofu 83
- Part 2 85

Introduction 86

Chapter 1 – Chinese Stir Fry 101 87

Chapter 2 – Stir-Fried Noodles And Rice 89

Beef Chow Fun.. 89

Shrimp Fried Rice 93

Mandarin Fried Rice.. 95

Chicken Chow Mein 97

Vegetarian Fried Rice 100

Roast Pork Lo Mein 102

Yangzhou Fried Rice 104

Chapter 3 - Vegan And Vegetarian Stir Fried Dishes. 107

Asparagus Tips and Bamboo Shoots 108

Hunan-Style Eggplant with Chopped Peanuts 110

Garlic Broccoli... 112

Glazed Five-Spice Carrots.. 113

Ginger-Garlic Baby Bok Choy 115

Buddha's Delight... 117

Ginger Veggie Stir Fry.. 120

Chapter 4 – Stir Fried Meat Dishes........................... 122

Chicken Kung Pao.. 122

General Tso's Chicken 125

Sesame Chicken 130

Beef with Broccoli Stir Fry 134

Pork Or Beef Chop Suey 136

Easy Orange Chicken Stir Fry...................................... 139

Lettuce Wraps... 141

Moo Goo Gai Pan.. 144

Mongolian Beef 146

Sweet and Sour Pork.. 148

Chapter 5 – Stir Fried Seafood Dishes 151

Garlic Pepper Crabs.. 151

Shrimp With Lobster Sauce 153

Chili Shrimp... 157

Fish Steaks in Black Bean Sauce 159

Seafood and Eggplant ..... **Error! Bookmark not defined.**

Conclusion 161

Part 1

Introduction

Get ready to cook a mouthwatering assortment of delicious Chinese recipes for any meal. Yes, that's right. The Essential Kitchen Series delivers a wonderful collection of unique recipes in one quick purchase. You'll get an assortment of fried rice recipes, which can easily be made at home. They're all here in one fantastic bundle. Enjoy a host of recipes that will simplify meal planning, save you time, and help you enjoy something delicious.

This cookbook is packed with so much fun and flavor that you'll be amazed at what you can create. Just take a look at some of the vibrant recipes we've included:

Chinese Style Chili Beef

Shrimp with Slaw

Crispy Wontons

Chinese Egg Soup

There is literally no way to go wrong with these wonderful recipes.

There really is no better way to prepare a nutritious rice recipe than as described in the pages of this masterful recipe collection. Inside this unusually simple guide, you'll learn how to make the most of your time, utilizing fresh ingredients, sensational spices, and robust flavors.

If you've ever wanted to step outside the norm and try something different, this is the recipe collection intended for you. Where else will you learn to make so many different fried rice dishes in a single download? Bring a new blend of unique flavors into your kitchen and make some delicious Chinese today!

Stir Fry Sichuan Style Prawns

Makes: 4 servings

Ingredients:

1½ tablespoons groundnut oil

1 finely chopped spring onion

1 tablespoon finely chopped ginger

2 minced garlic cloves

1 pound raw prawns

1 tablespoon tomato puree

2 teaspoons golden caster sugar

3 teaspoons chili bean sauce

2 teaspoons Chinese black vinegar

1 teaspoon cider vinegar

2 teaspoons sesame oil

½ teaspoon salt

½ teaspoon freshly ground black pepper

1 tablespoon coriander leaves, to serve

2 tablespoons sliced spring onion

Procedure:

In a large skillet, heat oil on medium heat.

Add spring onions, ginger and garlic and stir fry for about 20 seconds.

Add prawns and stir fry for about 1 minute.

Add tomato puree, golden caster sugar, chili bean sauce, Chinese black vinegar, cider vinegar, sesame oil, salt and ground black pepper and stir fry for about 3 to 4 minutes.

Top with the coriander and spring onion.

Chicken Chow Mein

Makes: 4 servings

Ingredients:

9 ounces egg noodles

2 tablespoons oil

1 tablespoon sesame oil

2 minced garlic cloves

1 pound cut into thin strips, chicken breasts

1 thinly sliced green red pepper

1 can tinned sweet corn

3 tablespoons light soy sauce

½ teaspoon salt

½ teaspoon freshly ground black pepper

¼ cup cut into thin strips spring onions

Procedure:

Bring water to a boil in a pan on high heat. Reduce heat to medium.

Add noodles and cook for about 4 to 5 minutes until tender.

Drain.

Place in the cold water.

In a large skillet, heat oil on medium heat.

Add garlic and stir fry for about 30 seconds.

Add chicken and stir fry for about 4 to 5 minutes until tender.

Remove from the pan and set aside.

Add green bell pepper and stir fry for about 4 to 5 minutes until tender.

Add sweet corn, soya sauce, salt and pepper and stir fry for about 1 to 2 minutes until tender.

Add spring onions and stir fry for about 1 minute until done.

Beef with Oyster Sauce

Makes: 4 servings

Ingredients:

1 pound cut into strips beef

1 tablespoon light soy sauce

1 tablespoon dark soy sauce

2 teaspoons sesame oil

1 tablespoon dry sherry

2 teaspoons corn flour

1 ½ tablespoons water

3 tablespoons groundnut oil

1 seeded and thinly sliced red bell pepper

1 seeded and thinly sliced green bell pepper

3 tablespoons oyster sauce

¼ cup chopped spring onions

Procedure:

In a bowl, add beef, light soya sauce, dark soya sauce, sesame oil and dry sherry mix to combine.

Cover and marinate for 20 to 30 minutes.

In a small bowl, mix together corn flour and water.

Set aside.

In a large skillet, heat groundnut oil on medium heat.

Add beef and stir fry for 4 to 5 minutes until browned.

Remove from the skillet and set aside.

Add red and green bell peppers and stir fry for about 3 to 4 minutes until tender.

Return the beef to the skillet and toss them with the oyster sauce.

Add corn flour mixture and cook for 2 to 3 minutes until thickened.

Top with spring onions.

Serve immediately.

Cashew Chicken

Makes: 4 servings

Ingredients:

1 pound cubed boneless, skinless chicken breasts

1 teaspoon sesame oil

2 teaspoons corn flour

1 egg white

½ teaspoon salt

½ teaspoon freshly ground black pepper

2 teaspoons groundnut oil

¼ cup cashew nuts

1 tablespoon dry sherry

1 tablespoon rice wine

1 tablespoon light soy sauce

¼ cup shredded spring onion

Procedure:

In a bowl, mix together chicken, sesame oil, corn flour, egg white, salt and pepper.

Leave for 30 minutes at room temperature.

In a large skillet, heat 1 teaspoon groundnut oil on medium heat.

Add chicken and cook for about 4 to 5 minutes until browned.

Transfer to a plate.

Heat remaining 1 teaspoon oil in the same skillet.

Add cashew nuts and cook for about 1 minute.

Add dry sherry, rice wine and soy sauce and cook for 1 to 2 minutes until thickened.

Return the chicken to the skillet and cook for about 2 to 3 minutes.

Top with spring onions.

Serve immediately.

Chinese Pork Balls

Makes: 4 servings

Ingredients:

1 pound minced lean pork

1 teaspoon Chinese five-spice powder

2 tablespoons soy sauce

2 tablespoons corn flour

1 can drained and chopped water chestnuts

½ teaspoon salt

½ teaspoon freshly ground black pepper

2 cups chicken broth

1 teaspoon shredded ginger

3 tablespoons hoisin sauce

2 peeled and strips, carrots

1 cup shredded Chinese leaves

½ cup bean sprouts

½ cup chopped spring onions

Procedure:

In a large bowl, mix together Chinese five-spice powder, soy sauce, corn flour, water chestnuts, salt and pepper and shape into small balls.

Pour the broth into a large skillet.

Add meatballs, ginger, hoisin sauce and mix well.

Cover and cook for about 5 to 7 minutes.

Add carrots, Chinese leaves, bean sprouts and spring onions and cook for about 4 to 5 minutes until done.

Chinese Five Spice Chicken Thighs

Makes: 8 servings

Ingredients:

2 pounds chicken thighs

4 teaspoons five spice powder

4 tablespoons groundnut oil

6 minced garlic cloves

1 teaspoon grated ginger

4 tablespoons dry sherry

4 tablespoons light soy sauce

4 tablespoons clear honey

1 cup chopped spring onions

Procedure:

Preheat the oven to 180 degrees C.

In a large bowl, mix together chicken, five spice powder, groundnut oil, garlic, ginger, dry sherry, soy sauce, honey, salt and pepper.

Transfer to the baking dish.

Bake for 35 to 40 minutes until done.

Top with spring onions.

Serve immediately.

Fried Rice with Prawn

Makes: 2 servings

Ingredients:

2 cups water

1 cup rice

2 tablespoons sesame oil

1 egg, beaten

1 minced garlic clove

½ cup chopped chorizo

¼ pound peeled prawns

½ seeded and chopped red bell pepper

¼ cup frozen peas

¼ teaspoon five spice powder

1 teaspoon soy sauce

½ teaspoon salt

½ teaspoon freshly ground black pepper

3 sliced spring onions

¼ cup bean sprouts

Procedure:

Bring water to a boil in a pan on high heat.

Add rice and cook for about 4 to 5 minutes until tender and water has been absorbed.

Turn off the heat and cover for about 10 minutes.

In a large skillet, heat 1 tablespoon oil on medium heat.

Add egg and cook for about 3 to 4 minutes until scrambled.

Transfer to the plate and set aside.

Heat remaining 1 tablespoon oil in the same skillet.

Add garlic and Chorizo and cook for 2 to 3 minutes.

Add prawns and cook for 4 to 5 minutes until tender.

Add red bell pepper and peas and cook for about 4 to 5 minutes until vegetables are tender.

Add five spice, rice, soy, salt and pepper and cook for about 4 to 5 minutes more.

Add spring onion, bean sprouts, egg and cook for about 4 to 5 minutes until heated through.

Stir Fried Greens

Makes: 3 servings

Ingredients:

½ cup vermicelli rice noodles

2 tablespoons sunflower oil

4 chopped spring onions

3 minced garlic cloves

¼ pound thinly sliced shiitake mushrooms

1 seeded and chopped red chili

2 cups broccoli florets

1 cup chopped Pak Choi

1 tablespoon soy sauce

1 teaspoon fish sauce

3 tablespoons oyster sauce

½ teaspoon salt

½ teaspoon freshly ground black pepper

Procedure:

Soak vermicelli rice noodles in the hot water for about 3 to 4 minutes until tender.

Pour the noodles into a colander to drain the water away.

In a large skillet, heat oil on medium heat.

Add spring onion and garlic and cook for 1 to 2 minutes until tender.

Add mushrooms and red chili and cook for about 5 to 6 minutes until tender.

Add the broccoli florets and Pak Choi and cook for about 4 to 5 minutes until vegetables are tender.

Add vermicelli rice noodles and cook for 4 to 5 minutes until heated through.

Add soy sauce, fish sauce, oyster sauce, salt and pepper and cook for about 1 to 2 minutes until thickened.

Tofu & Hazelnut with Noodles

Makes: 4 servings

Ingredients:

250 grams packet medium egg noodle

2 tablespoons sesame oil

¼ cup Mange tout

1 seeded and chopped red chili

¼ cup toasted hazelnuts, roughly chopped

½ pound cubed silken tofu

3 tablespoons Chinese yellow bean sauce

½ teaspoon salt

½ teaspoon freshly ground black pepper

Procedure:

Bring water to a boil in a pan on high heat.

Add noodles and cook for 1 to 2 minutes on medium heat until tender.

Pour the noodles into a colander to drain the water away.

Add a few drops of oil and toss to coat and set aside.

In a large skillet, heat oil on medium heat.

Add the mange tout and cook for about 1 to 2 minutes until tender.

Add the chili and cook for about 1 minute.

Add hazelnuts, tofu, yellow bean sauce, salt and pepper and cook for about 2 to 3 minutes until done.

Serve with the noodles.

Egg Fried Rice

Makes: 4 servings

Ingredients:

2 cups water

1 cup rice

2 tablespoons sunflower oil

2 large eggs

2 thinly sliced spring onions

2 thinly sliced garlic cloves

1 cup chopped back bacon rashers

1 chopped red bell pepper

1 teaspoon Chinese five-spice powder

½ teaspoon salt

½ teaspoon freshly ground black pepper

Procedure:

Bring water to a boil in a pan on high heat.

Add rice and cook for about 4 to 5 minutes until tender and water has been absorbed.

Turn off the heat and cover for about 10 minutes and set aside.

In a large skillet, heat 1 tablespoon oil on medium heat.

Add eggs and cook for about 3 to 4 minutes until scrambled.

Transfer to the plate and set aside.

Heat remaining 1 tablespoon oil in the same skillet.

Add spring onions and garlic and cook for 1 minute until tender.

Add back bacon rashers and cook for about 4 to 5 minutes until crispy.

Add red bell pepper and cook for 1 to 2 minutes until tender.

Add rice, scrambled egg, Chinese five-spice powder, salt and pepper and cook for about 4 to 5 minutes until heated through.

Ginger & Garlic Pork

Makes: 4 servings

Ingredients:

1 tablespoon sesame oil

2 minces garlic cloves

2 tablespoons shredded ginger

4 sliced spring onion

1 pound cut into strips, pork loin steaks

4 tablespoons hoisin sauce

½ pound sliced bokchoy

Procedure:

In a large skillet, heat oil on medium heat.

Add garlic and ginger and cook for 2 to 3 minutes until tender.

Add spring onion and cook for 1 minutes.

Add pork, salt and pepper and cook for 8 to 10 minutes until tender.

Add hoisin sauce and bok choy and cook for 4 to 5 until tender.

Sweet & Sour Chicken

Makes: 4 servings

Ingredients:

For the sauce:

¼ cup pineapple juice

3 tablespoons soy sauce

3 tablespoons white wine vinegar

3 tablespoons sherry

1 tablespoon light soft brown sugar

1 teaspoon corn flour

For batter:

1¼ cups self-rising flour

2 tablespoons oil

2 tablespoons corn flour

1 egg

1½ cups water

¼ teaspoon salt

¼ teaspoon white pepper

For Frying:

2 cups oil

For chicken:

1 pound cubed large skinless, boneless chicken breasts

3 teaspoons sesame oil

2 minced garlic cloves

2 teaspoons grated fresh ginger

1 seeded and thinly sliced red bell pepper

1 thinly sliced carrot

Procedure:

Make sauce; in a nonstick pan, add pineapple juice, soy sauce, white wine vinegar, sherry and sugar and cook for 2 to 3 minutes until sugar is dissolved.

Add corn flour and cook for 1 minute until thickened.

Remove from the heat and set aside.

In a bowl, mix together flour, oil, corn flour, egg, water, salt and white pepper until thick batter.

Add chicken pieces and mix until chicken is well coated.

In a large skillet, heat oil on medium heat.

Add chicken and fry for about 10 minutes until crisp and golden browned.

Set aside.

In another skillet, heat 3 tablespoons oil on medium heat.

Add garlic and ginger and sauté for about 1 to 2 minutes until tender.

Add red bell pepper and carrot and cook for about 2 to 3 minutes until vegetables are tender.

Add chicken and mix to combine.

Pour over sauce and cook for about 1 minute until done.

Kale with Oyster sauce

Makes: 2 servings

Ingredients:

1 tablespoon sesame oil

1 minced garlic clove

1 ½ cups chopped kale

¼ cup water

1 tablespoon soy sauce

1 tablespoon oyster sauce

¼ teaspoon salt

¼ teaspoon freshly ground black pepper

Procedure:

In a large skillet, heat oil on medium heat.

Add garlic and sauté for 1 minute.

Add kale and cook for 4 to 5 minutes until tender.

Add water, soy sauce, oyster sauce, salt and pepper.

Cover and cook for 6 to 7 minutes until thickened.

Chinese Steamed Bass

Makes: 2 servings

Ingredients:

½ pound sea bass fillets

½ teaspoon salt

½ teaspoon ground black pepper

2 teaspoons soy sauce

2 minced garlic cloves

1 teaspoon chopped ginger

1 seeded and chopped red chili

2 teaspoons sesame oil

½ cup sliced spring onion

Procedure:

Season fish with salt and pepper.

Cover and marinate for 2 hours.

Place the bass fillets on the platter.

Set the platter on the top of the Chinese bamboo steamer.

Cover and steam over boiling water 10 to 15 minutes.

In a bowl, mix together soy sauce, oil, garlic, ginger and red chili.

Set aside.

In a skillet, heat oil on medium heat.

Add spring onion and sauté for 3 to 4 minutes until tender.

Add soy sauce mixture and cook for 1 minutes.

Pour over the sea bass fillets.

Crispy Chinese pork

Makes: 4 servings

Ingredients:

1½ pounds pork belly

1 teaspoon Chinese five spice powder

2 teaspoons salt

For sauce:

4 tablespoons soy sauce

1 tablespoon Thai sweet chili sauce

1 tablespoon grated ginger

1 chopped spring onion

Procedure:

Preheat the oven to 350 F.

Season pork belly with Chinese five spice powder and salt.

Transfer to the refrigerator for at least 2 to 3 hours.

Place the pork belly on a wire rack.

Roast for 1 ½ hours.

Turn up the heat to 465 F.

Roast for another 30 to 40 minutes until crispy.

Make sauce; in a bowl, mix together all sauce ingredients.

Place pork on cutting board and rest for at least 10 minutes.

After that, cut into small pieces.

Serve with sauce.

Baked Chinese Wings

Makes: 4 servings

Ingredients:

1½ pounds large chicken wings

½ teaspoon sesame oil

4 minced garlic cloves

1 tablespoon grated ginger

½ teaspoon five spice powder

2 tablespoons lemon juice

2 tablespoons red wine

¼ cup soy sauce

2 tablespoons brown sugar

¼ cup tomato sauce

2 tablespoons hoisin sauce

2 tablespoons oyster sauce

2 tablespoons sambal oelek

For Toping:

2 tablespoons chopped spring onion

1 tablespoon sesame seeds

Procedure:

Preheat the oven to 350 degrees F.

In a bowl, mix together all ingredients until coated well.

Cover and leave for at least 30 minutes.

Transfer to the baking sheet.

Bake for 49 to 50 minutes until golden browned.

Top with spring onion and sesame seed.

Chinese Style Chilli Beef

Makes: 4 servings

Ingredients:

2 cups oil for deep frying

2 eggs, beaten

½ teaspoon salt

1 ½ tablespoons corn flour

½ pound cut into strips, beef steak

2 tablespoons sesame oil

2 shredded spring onions

2 minced garlic cloves, finely chopped

1 shredded carrot

1 chopped red chili

2 teaspoons sugar

2 tablespoons white rice vinegar

2 tablespoons sweet chili dipping sauce

1 teaspoon dark soy sauce

3 tablespoons oyster sauce

Procedure:

In a bowl, mix together egg, corn flour and salt until smooth.

Add beef and mix to combine.

In a large pan, heat oil on medium heat.

Add beef and fry for 10 minutes until crispy and golden browned.

Remove from pan and set aside.

In a large skillet, heat oil on medium heat.

Add spring onion and garlic and cook for about 2 to 3 minutes until tender.

Add carrot, red chili, sugar, white rice vinegar, sweet chili sauce, soy sauce and oyster sauce and mix together.

Add beef and cook 4 to 5 minutes until heated through.

Shrimp with Slaw

Makes: 6 servings

Ingredients:

For Slaw:

4 teaspoons sesame oil

¼ cup lime juice

4 teaspoons soy sauce

1 teaspoon sugar

6 cups thinly sliced cabbage

1 thinly sliced red bell pepper

1 thinly sliced orange bell pepper

For Shrimp:

¼ cup cornstarch

1 teaspoon five-spice powder

½ teaspoon salt

1 teaspoon freshly ground black pepper

1½ pounds peeled and deveined raw shrimp

2 tablespoons oil

2 seeded and minced jalapeno peppers

Procedure:

In a bowl, mix together sesame oil, lime juice, soy sauce, cabbage, red bell pepper and orange bell pepper.

Set aside.

In another bowl, mix together cornstarch, five-spice powder, salt and pepper.

Add shrimp and toss to coat.

In a large skillet, heat oil on medium heat.

Add the shrimp and cook for about 3 to 4 minutes until tender.

Add jalapenos and cook for about 1 to 2 minutes until done.

Transfer to the serving plate.

Serve with the slaw.

Crispy Wontons

Makes: 12 servings

Ingredients:

½ pound ground beef

8 canned chopped water chestnuts

¼ cup chopped spring onions

1 tablespoon soy sauce

1 teaspoon cornstarch

½ teaspoon salt

½ teaspoon grated fresh ginger

1 (16 ounce) package wonton skins

1 cup oil for deep-frying

Procedure:

In a bowl, mix together beef, water chestnuts, scallion, soy sauce, cornstarch, salt and ginger.

Place 1 tablespoon beef mixture in center of each wonton skin and fold wonton to form a triangle.

Turn top of triangle down to meet fold and turnover and one corner with water and overlap opposite corner over moistened corner and press together firmly.

In a large skillet, heat oil on medium heat.

Add wontons fry for 3 to 4 minutes until crispy and browned.

Chinese Egg Soup

Makes: 4 servings

Ingredients:

3 tablespoons water

2 tablespoons corn starch

4 cups chicken broth

½ cup green peas

2 lightly beaten eggs

1 tablespoon chili sauce

1 tablespoon soy sauce

½ teaspoon salt

¼ teaspoon white pepper

Procedure:

In a small bowl, mix together water and corn flour until smooth.

Set aside.

Bring broth and peas to a boil in a large soup pan on high heat.

Reduce heat to medium.

Slowly add egg and cook for about 3 to 4 minutes until egg is fully cooked.

Add chili sauce and soy sauce and mix to combine.

Add the corn flour mixture and cook for about 4 to 5 minutes, stirring constantly.

Season with salt and pepper.

Top with spring onion.

Serve immediately.

Beef & Broccoli

Makes: 4 servings

Ingredients:

2 tablespoons corn flour

4 tablespoons water

2 cups broccoli florets

2 tablespoons sesame oil

½ pound cut into strips beef tenderloin

1 teaspoon grated ginger

½ tablespoon soy sauce

1 teaspoon sherry

1 tablespoon oyster sauce

½ teaspoon sugar

¼ teaspoon salt

¼ teaspoon white pepper

Procedure:

In a small bowl, mix together water and corn flour until smooth.

Set aside.

Bring the water to boil in a pan on high heat.

Reduce heat to medium.

Add broccoli florets and cook for about 1 to 2 minutes.

Drain and set aside.

In a large skillet, heat oil on medium heat.

Add beef and cook for 8 to 10 minutes until browned.

Add broccoli, ginger, soy sauce, sherry, oyster sauce, sherry, salt and pepper and mix to combine.

Add the corn flour mixture and cook for 2 to 3 minutes until lightly thickened.

Sweet & Sour Pork

Makes: 4 servings

Ingredients:

For the sauce:

¼ cup pineapple juice

3 tablespoons soy sauce

3 tablespoons white wine vinegar

3 tablespoons oyster sauce

1 tablespoon brown sugar

1 teaspoon corn flour

For batter:

1 ¼ cups self-rising flour

2 tablespoons oil

2 tablespoons cornstarch

1 egg

1 ½ cups water

¼ teaspoon salt

¼ teaspoon white pepper

For Frying:

2 cups oil

For chicken:

1 pound cubed pork tenderloin

3 teaspoons sesame oil

2 minced garlic cloves

2 teaspoons grated fresh ginger

1 seeded and thinly sliced green bell pepper

1 seeded and thinly sliced red bell pepper

1 cup cubed pineapple

Procedure:

Make sauce; in a nonstick pan, add pineapple juice, soy sauce, white wine vinegar, oyster sauce and sugar and cook for 2 to 3 minutes until sugar is dissolved.

Add corn flour and cook for 1 minute until thickened.

Remove from the heat and set aside.

In a bowl, mix together flour, oil, cornstarch, egg, water, salt and white pepper until thick batter.

Add pork and mix until chicken is well coated.

In a large skillet, heat oil on medium heat.

Add the pork and fry for about 10 minutes until crisp and golden browned.

Set aside.

In another skillet, heat 3 tablespoons oil on medium heat.

Add garlic and ginger and sauté for about 1 to 2 minutes until tender.

Add green bell pepper, red bell pepper and pineapple and cook for about 2 to 3 minutes until vegetables are tender.

Add pork and mix to combine.

Pour over sauce and cook for about 1 minute until done.

Kung Pao Chicken

Makes: 4 servings

Ingredients:

For Marinade:

1 pound cubed boneless & skinless chicken breasts

1 tablespoon corn flour

2 teaspoons soy sauce

1 tablespoon Chinese Shaoxing rice wine

For Sauce:

1½ tablespoon soy sauce

1 teaspoon sugar

¼ teaspoon Chinese black vinegar

2 tablespoons water

1 teaspoon corn flour

3 tablespoons sesame oil

1 teaspoon grated ginger

2 minced garlic cloves

1 chopped spring onion

3 tablespoons roasted peanuts

8 seeded and sliced dried red chilies

Procedure:

In a large bowl, add all ingredients and mix to combine.

Cover and marinade for 20 to 30 minutes.

Make sauce; in a bowl, mix together soy sauce, sugar, Chinese black vinegar, water and corn flour.

Set aside.

In a large skillet, heat sesame oil on medium heat.

Add chicken and cook for 8 to 10 minutes until tender.

Add garlic, ginger and spring onion and sauté for 2 to 3 minutes until tender.

Add peanuts, dried chili and sauce and cook for 4 to 5 minutes until thickened.

Orange Chicken

Makes: 4 servings

Ingredients:

1½ pounds cubed boneless, skinless chicken breasts

1 cup chicken broth

½ cup freshly squeezed orange juice

½ cup sugar

1/3 cup distilled white vinegar

¼ cup soy sauce

2 minced garlic cloves

1 tablespoon orange zest

1 teaspoon Sriracha

¼ teaspoon ground ginger

¼ teaspoon salt

¼ teaspoon white pepper

2 large eggs, beaten

1 cup corn flour

1 cup vegetable oil

½ teaspoon sesame seeds

1 sliced green onion

Procedure:

In a bowl, mix together chicken, chicken broth, orange juice, sugar, vinegar, soy sauce, garlic, orange zest, Sriracha, ginger, salt and white pepper.

Cover and marinade for 30 minutes.

Drain the chicken from the marinade and reserve the marinate

sauce.

Dip the chicken into the eggs and then coat with corn flour.

In a large skillet, heat oil on medium heat.

Add chicken and cook for about 2 to 3 minutes until golden browned.

Transfer to the bowl.

Pour over reserved marinate sauce.

Top with sesame seeds and green onion.

Pineapple Fried Rice

Makes: 4 servings

Ingredients:

2 cups water

1 cup rice

1 tablespoon sesame oil

1 sliced spring onion

1 minced garlic clove

1 teaspoon minced ginger

1 cup prawns

½ carrot, grated

1 seeded, cubed red bell pepper

2 teaspoons jalapeno peppers

8 canned cubed pineapple rings

½ teaspoon salt

½ teaspoon freshly ground black pepper

Procedure:

Bring water to a boil in a pan on high heat.

Add rice and cook for about 4 to 5 minutes until tender and water has been absorbed.

Turn off the heat and cover for about 10 minutes.

In a large skillet, heat oil on medium heat.

Add spring onion, garlic and ginger and cook for 2 to 3 minutes until tender.

Add prawns and cook for 4 to 5 minutes until tender.

Add carrot, red bell pepper and jalapeno peppers and cook for 2 to 3 minutes until vegetables are tender.

Season with salt and pepper.

Add rice and pineapple and mix to combine.

Serve immediately.

Chinese Pepper Steaks

Makes: 4 servings

Ingredients:

1 tablespoon corn flour

1½ tablespoon water

2 tablespoons sesame oil

1 minced garlic clove

1½ pounds cut into strips, beef steak

1 seeded and julienned red bell peppers

1 seeded and julienned green bell peppers

1 minced garlic clove

1 cups sliced mushrooms

¾ cup beef broth

¼ cup light soy sauce

2 teaspoons sugar

½ teaspoon salt

½ teaspoon white pepper

1 chopped spring onion

Procedure:

In a small bowl, mix together corn flour and water.

Set aside.

In a large skillet, heat oil on medium heat.

Add garlic and sauté for 1 minute.

Add steak and cook for 8 to 10 minutes until golden browned.

Add red and green bell peppers and cook for 2 to 3 minutes until tender.

Add mushrooms and cook for 5 to 6 minutes.

Add broth, soy sauce, sugar, salt and pepper and cook for 7 to 8 minutes.

Add the corn flour mixture and cook for 2 to 3 minutes until thickened.

Top with spring onion.

Baked Chicken Wings with Hoisin Sauce

Makes: 6 servings

Ingredients:

1½ pounds chicken wings

2 minced garlic cloves

1 teaspoon grated ginger

4 tablespoons hoisin sauce

1 tablespoon honey

3 tablespoons warm water

1 minced spring onion

¾ teaspoon salt

½ teaspoon black pepper

Procedure:

In a bowl, mix together chicken, wings, garlic, ginger, hoisin sauce, honey, water, spring onion, salt and pepper.

Cover and marinade for 30 to 40 minutes.

Preheat oven at 350 degrees F.

Bake for about 30 to 35 minutes until golden browned.

Chicken with Bok Choy

Makes: 4 servings

Ingredients:

For sauce:

1 tablespoon rice vinegar

¼ cup low sodium soy sauce

3 tablespoons water

2 teaspoons light brown sugar

For Chicken:

1 pound cut into strips boneless, skinless chicken breasts

4 teaspoons corn flour

2 tablespoons vegetable oil

2 minced garlic cloves

2 teaspoons minced fresh ginger

4 cups sliced bok Choy

1 seeded and sliced jalapeno

Procedure:

In a small bowl, mix together rice, vinegar, soy sauce, water and brown sugar.

Coat chicken strips with corn flour.

Set aside.

In a large skillet, heat oil on medium heat.

Add garlic and ginger and cook for about 1 minute.

Add chicken and cook for about 7 to 9 minutes until tender.

Add bok Choy and jalapeno and cook for about 1 to 2 minutes.

Add sauce and cook for 2 to 3 minutes until thickened.

Stir Fried Shrimp & Broccoli

Makes: 4 servings

Ingredients:

¾ pound peeled and deveined large shrimp

Salt and freshly ground black pepper

2 tablespoons sesame oil

1 minced clove garlic

1 sliced red onion

4 thinly sliced carrots

½ pound broccoli florets

¼ cup soy sauce

2 tablespoons honey

1 tablespoon corn flour

2 tablespoon water

Procedure:

Season chicken with salt and pepper.

In a large skillet, heat oil on medium heat.

Add shrimp and cook for 3 to 4 minutes until tender.

Remove from the pan and set aside.

Add garlic, onion, carrot and broccoli to the skillet and cook for 4 to 5 minutes until vegetables are tender.

Return shrimp to the pan.

Add soy sauce, honey, corn flour and water and cook for 1 minute until thickened.

Vegetables, Fried Rice

Makes: 4 servings

Ingredients:

1½ cups white rice

3 tablespoons sesame oil

4 eggs, beaten

2 thinly sliced carrots

2 cups cut into thirds snow peas

2 cups bean sprouts

4 thinly sliced spring onions

¾ cup soy sauce

2 tablespoons light brown sugar

1 tablespoon rice vinegar

1 tablespoon grated fresh ginger

½ teaspoon salt

Procedure:

Bring water to a boil in a pan on high heat.

Add rice and cook for about 4 to 5 minutes until tender and water has been absorbed.

Turn off the heat and cover for about 10 minutes.

In a large skillet, heat 2 tablespoons oil on medium heat.

Add egg and cook for about 2 to 3 minutes until scrambled.

Transfer to the plate and set aside.

Heat remaining 1 tablespoon oil in the same skillet.

Add the carrots and cook for about 2 to 3 minutes.

Add snow peas, bean sprouts and spring onions and cook for about 2 to 3 minutes until vegetables are tender.

Add soy sauce, sugar, vinegar, and ginger and cook for about 1 to 2 minutes.

Add rice and scramble egg and mix to combine.

Cover and cook for 4 to 5 minutes on low heat until heated through.

Sesame Noodles

Makes: 4 servings

Ingredients:

12 ounces spaghetti noodles

2 tablespoons sesame oil

4 minced garlic cloves

2 cups chopped broccoli florets

¼ cup finely chopped red bell peppers

3 chopped spring onions

¼ cup soy sauce

1 tablespoon honey

1/8 teaspoon crushed red pepper flakes

¼ teaspoon salt

1 tablespoon sesame seeds

Procedure:

Bring water to a boil in a pan on high heat.

Reduce heat to medium.

Add noodles and cook for about 4 to 5 minutes until tender.

Drain and set aside.

In a large skillet, heat oil on medium heat.

Add garlic and sauté for 1 minute.

Add broccoli and cook for about 4 to 5 minutes until tender.

Add red bell pepper and spring onions and cook for about 2 to 3 minutes.

Add noodles, soy sauce, honey, red pepper flakes and salt and cook for 1 to 2 minutes until done.

Top with sesame seeds.

Chinese Chicken Salad

Makes: 4 servings

Ingredients:

2 cups romaine lettuce

3 cups shredded rotisserie chicken

2 cans drained, mandarin oranges

2 cups cooked chow Mein noodles

For Dressing:

¼ cup peanut butter

1 tablespoon chili garlic sauce

1 teaspoon garlic powder

1 teaspoon honey

¼ cup hoisin sauce

3 tablespoons canola oil

3 tablespoons rice wine vinegar

Salt and freshly ground black pepper, to taste

Procedure:

In a large salad bowl, mix together lettuce, chicken, mandarin oranges and chow Mein noodles.

In a bowl, mix together the dressing ingredients.

Pour over the salad.

Stir Fry Sugar Snap Peas

Makes: 4 servings

Ingredients:

½ pound cubed boneless, skinless chicken breasts

1 tablespoon corn flour

1 egg white

1 tablespoon rice wine

2 tablespoons sesame oil

1 cup sliced sugar snap peas

¼ cup shredded carrots

2 teaspoons golden caster sugar

3 teaspoons chili bean sauce

2 teaspoons Chinese black vinegar

3 tablespoons oyster sauce

2 tablespoons teriyaki sauce

Procedure:

In a medium bowl, mix together chicken, corn flour, egg white and rice wine.

Let marinate for about 30 minutes at room temperature.

In a skillet, heat oil on medium heat.

Add chicken and cook for about 8 to 10 minutes until golden browned.

Add sugar snap peas, carrots, golden caster sugar, chili bean sauce, Chinese black vinegar and oyster sauce and cook for 4 to 5 minutes until crisp.

Add teriyaki sauce and cook for 2 to 3 minutes until done.

Salmon with Gingery Green Beans

Makes: 4 servings

Ingredients:

3 tablespoons sesame oil

1¼ pounds cubed skinless salmon fillet

4 thinly sliced spring onions

2 minced garlic cloves

1 tablespoon grated ginger

¾ pound trimmed green beans

2 teaspoons golden caster sugar

3 teaspoons chili bean sauce

2 teaspoons Chinese black vinegar

1 teaspoon cider vinegar

3 tablespoons oyster sauce

¼ teaspoon salt

2 tablespoons chili garlic sauce

Procedure:

In a large skillet, heat oil on medium heat.

Add fish and cook for 4 to 5 minutes until tender.

Remove from pan and set aside.

Add the scallions, garlic, and ginger to the pan and cook for about 1 minute.

Add the green beans, golden caster sugar, chili bean sauce, Chinese black vinegar, cider vinegar, oyster sauce and salt and cook for about 4 to 6 minutes until tender.

Serve salmon with green beans.

Drizzle with the chili garlic sauce.

Honey Prawns

Makes: 4 servings

Ingredients:

1 ½ cups water

1 egg, beaten

1 cup self-rising flour

½ cup corn flour

1 pound king prawns

Vegetable oil, for deep-frying

½ cup warmed honey

½ cup sesame seeds

Procedure:

In a bowl, mix together egg, water, self-rising flour and corn flour until smooth batter.

Dip prawns in batter and shaking off any excess.

In a large skillet, heat oil on medium heat.

Add prawns and fry for 3 to 4 minutes until golden browned.

Toss prawns with honey.

Sprinkle with sesame seeds.

Serve immediately.

Chinese Grilled Chicken

Makes: 2 servings

Ingredients:

½ pound boneless, skinless chicken breasts

¼ cup lemon juice

3 tablespoons olive oil

1 minced garlic clove

2 tablespoons hoisin sauce

1 tablespoon honey

5 tablespoons soy sauce

¼ teaspoon ground ginger

Procedure:

In a bowl, mix together all ingredients.

Cover and leave for at least4 to 5 hours.

Preheat the grill on medium.

Add chicken and grilled for about 4 to 5 minutes on each side.

Cut into slices and serve.

Corn Soup

Makes: 6 servings

Ingredients:

2 tablespoons corn flour

2 tablespoons water

2 cans low sodium chicken broth

2 cans cream-style corn

3 teaspoons chili sauce

2 teaspoons Chinese black vinegar

1 teaspoon cider vinegar

1 tablespoon oyster sauce

½ teaspoon salt

½ teaspoon freshly ground black pepper

2 eggs, beaten

Procedure:

In a bowl, mix together corn flour and water. Set aside. Bring broth to a boil on high heat. Reduce heat to medium.

Add cream-style corn, chili sauce, Chinese black vinegar, cider vinegar, oyster sauce, salt and pepper and cook for 2 to 3 minutes.

Slowly add egg and cook for about 3 to 4 minutes until egg is fully cooked.

Add the corn flour mixture and cook for 5 to 8 minutes on low heat until lightly thickened.

Hot & Sour Soup

Makes: 4 servings

Ingredients:

2 tablespoons corn flour

3 tablespoons of water

12 dried lily buds

½ cup dried mushrooms

8 cups low-sodium chicken broth

2 tablespoons white vinegar

2 tablespoons dark soy sauce

½ teaspoon salt

2 large eggs

½ cup shredded bamboo shoots

½ cup shredded cooked pork

1 cup shredded spiced thick and dry tofu

1½ teaspoons finely ground white pepper

1 tablespoon sesame oil

¼ cup chopped spring onion

Procedure:

In a small bowl, mix together corn flour with water until smooth.

Set aside.

In a bowl, add dried lily buds and cover with boiled water.

Leave for 10 to 15 minutes until tender.

After that, cut off the hard and discard the tough tips.

In another small bowl, cover the dried mushrooms with boiling water.

Leave for 25 to 30 minutes until tender.

Bring broth to a boil in a large soup pan.

Add the vinegar, soy sauce and salt and mix to combine.

Slowly add egg and cook for about 3 to 4 minutes until egg is fully cooked.

Add the lily buds, mushrooms, bamboo shoots, pork, tofu and white pepper and cook for about 4 to 5 minutes.

Add the corn flour mixture and cook for 5 to 8 minutes on low heat until lightly thickened.

Divide the soup 4 bowls.

Drizzle each with sesame oil.

Top with chopped spring onion.

Chinese Roasted Ribs

Makes: 2 servings

Ingredients:

1 pound pork ribs

5 minced garlic cloves

1 tablespoon minced sweet pineapple

2 tablespoons peanut oil

2 tablespoons hoisin sauce

1 teaspoon ground bean sauce

2 tablespoons tomato puree

5 tablespoons sugar

2 tablespoons honey

5 tablespoons ketchup

½ tablespoon five spice powder

2 tablespoons fresh squeezed orange juice

1 tablespoon salt

1 teaspoon fresh ground pepper

½ tablespoon paprika

Procedure:

In a large bowl, add all ingredients and mix to combine.

Cover and marinate for at least 4 to 5 hours.

Preheat the oven to 325 degrees F.

Place ribs on the baking sheet.

Roast for about 35 to 40 minutes.

Turning and brush with marinate mixture.

Bake or another 10 to 15 minutes until done.

Sautéed Green Beans

Makes: 4 servings

Ingredients:

2 tablespoons peanut oil

2 chopped spring onions

1 minced garlic clove

1 tablespoon grated ginger

1 pound trimmed green beans

½ teaspoon chili sauce

1 tablespoon dark soy sauce

½ teaspoon sugar

¼ teaspoon salt

¼ teaspoon white pepper

Procedure:

In a large skillet, heat oil on medium heat.

Add spring onions, garlic and ginger and sauté for 2 to 3 minutes.

Add green beans and sauté for about 6 to 7 minutes until tender.

Add chili sauce, dark soy sauce, sugar, salt and pepper and cook for 2 to 3 minutes until done.

Salt & Pepper Tofu

Makes: 2 servings

Ingredients:

1 block drained and cubed extra firm tofu

4 tablespoons corn flour

½ teaspoon salt

½ teaspoon freshly ground black pepper

1 cup vegetable oil for frying

½ tablespoon oil

1 minced garlic clove

1 tablespoon grated ginger

2 chopped leeks

1 chopped celery rib

1 chopped green bell pepper

1 tablespoon light soy sauce

1 tablespoon dark soy sauce

½ teaspoon brown sugar

3 teaspoons chili bean sauce

1 teaspoon cider vinegar

3 tablespoons oyster sauce

Procedure:

In a bowl, mix together corn flour, salt and pepper.

Add tofu and toss to coat.

In a large nonstick pan, heat1 cup vegetable oil on medium heat.

Add tofu and fry for 3 to 4 minutes until golden browned.

Set aside.

In a large skillet, heat oil on medium heat.

Add ginger and garlic and cook for about 1to 2 minutes.

Add leeks, celery, and green bell pepper and cook for about 2 minutes.

Add tofu, light soy sauce, dark soy sauce, brown sugar, chili sauce, cider vinegar, oyster sauce and cook for 2 to 3 minutes until done.

Part 2

Introduction

This book contains proven steps and strategies on how to prepare simple, easy, and tasty stir fry Chinese takeout dishes.

Are you tired of ordering Chinese take-outs without knowing what the exact ingredients are? Would you rather prepare Chinese stir fried dishes at home using fresh and healthy ingredients? Well then, this is the cookbook you're looking for!

This cookbook will teach you how to quickly prepare Chinese stir-fried meals that you so often order for takeout. Each recipe is guaranteed to be easy with ingredients that you can conveniently find in any local grocery store (with a Chinese food section).

Whenever you want to whip out that wok, all you should do is choose from the collection of noodle, rice, vegan and vegetarian, chicken, red meat, and seafood stir fried recipes.

Best of all, the recipes are good for two to three servings, so you can choose to cook for yourself and your partner, your friends, or for make-ahead meals. So, go ahead and impress them with homemade Chinese cuisine straight from your kitchen.

Thanks again for downloading this book, I hope you enjoy it!

Chapter 1 – Chinese Stir Fry 101

What is it about Chinese stir fried dishes that make them so mouth-wateringly sumptuous? One reason I can think of is that the wok can meld all the different ingredients and flavors into one dish.

Stir frying is an art form in Chinese cuisine, but you do not have to be a master chef to create your own delicious versions at home. To ensure the quality of flavor and presentation of each Chinese stir-fried dish you are about to prepare, be sure to master the following essentials:

Choose a good quality wok

You are likely to be cooking on a traditional stove, so pick a wok that best suits it. One such design is a flat-bottomed, carbon-steel or cast-iron wok that is approximately 12 to 14 inches in diameter.

Prepare the ingredients before cooking

Stir frying requires a lot of concentration to prevent over or undercooking your food. To avoid forgetting ingredients during the process and ensure that everything goes smoothly, prepare all the ingredients before lighting your fire. Chop the meat and vegetables uniformly, measure all spices and herbs and place them in appropriate containers, combine the sauces beforehand (unless otherwise stated in a recipe), and line them up right next to the stove.

Make sure that the vegetables you are using are completely drained; otherwise, your entire dish will be soggy. If you do not want to set the washed vegetables aside for hours in a colander, invest in a salad spinner. These are readily available in stores and online.

Heat the wok through before adding oil

It is important to heat the wok over a high flame until it is slightly smoking before you add the oil. As soon as the oil hits the wok, swirl it around to coat the base.

Cook bulk ingredients in batches

If you are cooking in bulk in a 14-inch wok, make sure you divide the meat and cook no more than 12 ounces at a time. As for vegetables, stir fry no more than 4 cups at a time. If you cook any more than that, you will end up with undercooked, steamed up soggy ingredients, instead of the crisp tender stir fried dish that you want.

Do not be too hard on yourself if your dish does go to plan on your first attempt. It takes a lot of practice to develop the stir frying technique. Just practice whenever you can and choose the healthiest ingredients that your food budget allows.

Chapter 2 – Stir-Fried Noodles And Rice

Beef Chow Fun

This rice noodle dish comes from Canton and is usually served in *yum cha* restaurants located in the city of Guangdong, Hong Kong. It can also be found abroad in *cha chaan tengs*. The term chow fun or chow fun noodles is normally used to refer to many different dishes, the core ingredient of which is *chow fun* or *hor fun* noodles (wide rice noodles). You will also find it referred to as *Shahe fen*. These noodles come from the town of Shahe, located in the Guangzhou province of China. There are two ways to fry *hor fun* – dry fry (without sauce) or wet fry (with sauce).

The origins of these noodles are unknown. However, the origin of dry fried *hor fun* does exist in local legend. The legend states that a man called Mr. Hui left Canton for the province of Hunan during World War II to become a chef. One night, the stall that Mr. Hui had opened ran out of powder, a similar powder to corn-starch used as a thickening agent in sauces. A military commander wanted wet fried *chow fun*. Once he was informed that it wouldn't be possible, the commander lost his temper and started waving his gun around. Afraid that he would kill someone, Mr. Hui's mother and brother decided to prepare *tong yuen* or sticky rice dumplings. That was when Mr. Hui thought to dry fry the noodles. The preparation pleased the commander enough that Mr. Hui, his family and business were spared.

Try to keep in mind when cooking this dish that it must be cooked on a high heat and should be stirred quickly. However, while stirring the *hor fun* be careful not to exert too much pressure or the noodles will break. Another factor to keep in mind is the amount of oil you use. If there is too much oil it could ruin the noodles.

Serves 2

Ingredients:

- 1 ½ Tbsp. vegetable or peanut oil
- ¼ lb. flank steak, sliced into thin strips against the grain
- 6 oz. wide dried rice noodles
- 1 cup fresh bean sprouts
- ½ Tbsp. fermented black beans
- 1 tsp minced fresh ginger
- 1 tsp minced garlic
- 1 ½ scallions, julienned
- Freshly ground black pepper

For the Marinade:

- ½ Tbsp. soy sauce

- ½ Tbsp. dry sherry or Chinese rice wine
- ½ tsp corn starch

For the Seasoning:

- 1 ½ Tbsp. dry sherry or Chinese rice wine
- 1 Tbsp. oyster sauce
- ½ tsp sugar
- 1 tsp sesame oil

Instructions:

1. Combine all the ingredients for the marinade in a bowl. Add the chopped flank steak and turn several times to coat. Set aside to marinate.
2. In another bowl, combine all the ingredients for the seasoning and set aside.
3. Place the fermented black beans in a small bowl, then add water. Rinse and drain thoroughly, then mash and set aside.
4. Prepare the dried noodles per package instructions.
5. Place the wok over medium high flame and add half the oil. Swirl to coat.
6. Add the ginger and garlic then stir fry until fragrant. Add the beef and sear for 1 minute; do not touch.
7. Add the mashed black beans and stir fry until the beef is coated all over. Transfer to a plate and set aside.

8. Wipe the wok dry with paper towels, then heat the remaining oil. Swirl to coat.

9. Add the noodles and spread out into a single layer. Set to high flame and cook, untouched, for 45 seconds or until crisp.

10. Stir in the bean sprouts and scallions until tender, then add the beef mixture and the seasoning mixture. Stir fry until the beef is cooked through.

11. Mix everything well, then season to taste with pepper. Transfer to a takeout style box or serving dish, then serve right away.

Shrimp Fried Rice

Ingredients

- 4 oz. frozen uncooked and unshelled shrimp
- 4 oz. cooked ham
- 2 green onions
- 1 medium onion
- 2 eggs (you can use more if you want)
- 4 cups cold cooked rice
- ½ cup peas
- 4-5 Tbsp. oil for stir frying

For the marinade

- 1 Tbsp. soy sauce
- 1 Tbsp. oyster sauce
- Pepper to taste
- 1 tsp salt
- 1 tsp corn starch mixed with 1 ½ tsp water

Instructions

1. Run the frozen shrimp under running water.
2. Pat dry with paper towels and then shell the shrimp.
3. Chop the shrimp into small pieces.
4. Add the ingredients for the marinade and marinate the shrimp for about fifteen minutes.

5. Dice the green onion, onion, and ham.
6. Beat the eggs lightly with a pair of chopsticks.
7. Add some salt to the eggs. Set aside.
8. Heat the wok over a high flame.
9. Add 1 tablespoon of oil.
10. Once the oil is hot, add half of the egg mixture to the wok.
11. Cook the mix over a medium heat, turning the eggs over once.
12. Repeat with the remainder of the eggs.
13. Cut the eggs into thin strips. Set aside.
14. Heat 2 tablespoons of oil in the wok.
15. Once the oil is hot, stir fry the onion and shrimp on a high flame for a little while, then set aside.
16. Repeat the same procedure for the diced ham and green peas.
17. In the wok, add one to two tablespoons of oil.
18. Once it's hot, add the cooked rice, a bit of soy sauce and/or oyster sauce. Stir fry.
19. Add everything else, except the green onion and eggs. Mix well.
20. Serve the rice with the eggs and green onion as garnish.

Mandarin Fried Rice

Makes 2 servings

Ingredients:

- 1 Tbsp. vegetable or peanut oil
- 2 cups leftover cooked white rice
- 1 egg, beaten
- ½ Chinese sausage, diced
- 1 Tbsp. minced ginger
- 1 Tbsp. minced garlic
- ¼ cup chopped scallions
- 1 Tbsp. soy sauce
- ½ tsp sesame oil
- Sea salt
- Freshly ground black pepper

Instructions:

1. Moisten the rice with some water and break up. Set aside.
2. Beat the egg in a bowl until foamy. Set aside.
3. Place the wok over a medium-high flame and add half the vegetable or peanut oil. Swirl to coat.

4. Pour in the egg and cook for 30 seconds per side. Mince, then set aside on a plate.

5. Heat half the remaining oil, then swirl to coat. Stir in the shrimp and cook for 2 minutes, or until cooked through. Transfer to a plate and set aside.

6. Heat half the remaining oil, then swirl to coat. Stir in the Chinese sausage and stir fry until cooked through. Transfer to a plate and set aside.

7. Add the remaining oil and stir fry the garlic and ginger until fragrant. Add the rice, soy sauce, and scallions, then stir fry until dry and completely loosened.

8. Stir in the Chinese sausage and egg. Stir fry until rice is golden.

9. Season to taste with salt and pepper, then fold in the sesame oil. Transfer to a takeout style box or serving dish, then serve right away.

Chicken Chow Mein

Chow mein is the corrupted English version of chāu-mèing, a Taishanese term that means fried noodles. The dish is popular throughout China. Outside, countries such as the United States of America, Nepal, Britain, and India have taken to it with a lot of enthusiasm. The dish has evolved in each of these places until it bears only some resemblance to the original. Different regions in China originally cooked chow mein noodles in different styles. Some areas would fry the noodles until they were crispy, while other places steamed them to keep them soft. Even in America different regions prefer the two different preparations. Typically, the east coast cooks them crispier, while the west coast prefers to steam them.

Serves 2

Ingredients:

- 1 ½ Tbsp. vegetable or peanut oil
- ¼ lb. boneless, skinless chicken breast, sliced into thin strips
- 1 small onion, sliced thinly
- ½ small green bell pepper, julienned
- ½ cup fresh bean sprouts
- 1 small carrot, julienned
- 3 dried shiitake mushrooms
- 5 oz. thin dried Chinese egg noodles

For the Marinade:

- ½ Tbsp. soy sauce
- ¼ Tbsp. dry sherry or Chinese rice wine

For the Sauce:

- 2 ½ Tbsp. chicken broth
- ½ Tbsp. hoisin sauce
- ¾ Tbsp. soy sauce
- Freshly ground or white pepper

Instructions:

1. Place the shiitake mushrooms in a bowl, add warm water. Set aside for 20 minutes to soak.
2. After 20 minutes, drain the mushrooms and press out as much excess water as possible with paper towels.
3. Trim off the mushroom stems and chop the caps thinly. Set aside.
4. Combine the marinade mixture in a bowl, then add the chicken and toss to coat. Set aside for 15 minutes.
5. Meanwhile, boil a pot of water, add the noodles and cook based on package instructions. Drain and rinse under cold running water. Set aside to drain in a colander.
6. Combine all the ingredients for the sauce. Set aside.

7. Place the wok over a medium-high flame and add half the oil. Swirl to coat.
8. Stir in the chicken until browned, then stir in the bell pepper, carrot, onion, mushrooms, and bean sprouts. Carefully stir fry for 2 minutes, or until the chicken is cooked through.
9. Transfer the mixture onto a platter. Set aside.
10. Pour in the remaining oil and stir fry the noodles until golden. Create a pit in the center of the noodles and pour in the sauce.
11. Stir the chicken and vegetable mixture back into the wok with the noodles. Stir fry until combined.
12. Transfer to a takeout style box or serving dish, then serve right away.

Vegetarian Fried Rice

Serves 2

Ingredients:

- 1 Tbsp. vegetable oil
- 2 cups leftover cooked white rice
- ½ Tbsp. minced garlic
- 1 Tbsp. minced fresh chilies
- 2 ½ Tbsp. chopped shallots
- ½ cup diced carrot
- ¼ cup diced celery
- ¼ cup diced red bell pepper
- 1 Tbsp. chopped fresh cilantro
- ½ Tbsp. soy sauce
- 1 tsp sesame oil
- Sea salt
- Freshly ground black pepper

Instructions:

1. Moisten the rice with some water and break up. Set aside.
2. Place the wok over a medium high flame and add the vegetable or peanut oil. Swirl to coat.

3. Stir in the chilies, garlic and shallots and stir fry for 5 seconds. Stir in the carrots and reduce to medium flame. Stir fry until tender.

4. Stir in the celery, bell pepper, rice and soy sauce. Increase to medium high flame and stir fry until rice is dry and completely loosened.

5. Season to taste with salt and pepper, then fold in the cilantro and sesame oil.

6. Transfer to a takeout style box or serving dish, then serve right away.

Roast Pork Lo Mein

Lo mein is a Chinese noodle dish made from wheat flour noodles. It is not usually cooked with pork and instead uses either vegetables, chicken or seafood. Originally, this was a different type of wonton noodle soup. When served, the soup is strained from the rest of the ingredients and the noodles are served as a side dish. Lo mein is a variant of the Cantonese term lōu mihn which means stirred noodles.

Serves 2

Ingredients:

- ½ Tbsp. vegetable or peanut oil
- ¼ lb. Chinese barbecued pork, chopped into bite-sized chunks
- 6 oz. dried Chinese egg noodles
- ¾ tsp minced garlic
- 2 scallions, chopped
- ½ tsp minced fresh ginger
- 2 fresh shiitake mushrooms, sliced thinly
- 1 Tbsp. sesame oil

For the Sauce:

- 1 ½ Tbsp. soy sauce
- ¾ Tbsp. dry sherry or Chinese rice wine

- ¾ Tbsp. oyster sauce
- ¾ tsp honey

Instructions:

1. Cook the noodles based on package instructions, then drain and rinse under cold running water. Set aside in a colander.
2. Meanwhile, combine the ingredients for the sauce in a bowl, then set aside.
3. Place the noodles in a bowl and add the sesame oil. Toss to coat, then set aside.
4. Place the wok over a medium high flame and add half the vegetable or peanut oil. Swirl to coat.
5. Stir fry the ginger, garlic and scallions until fragrant. Stir in the mushrooms and stir fry until tender.
6. Add the pork and stir fry until well done. Add the noodles and sauce, then stir fry until combined.
7. Transfer to a takeout style box or serving dish, then serve right away.

Yangzhou Fried Rice

This dish is also known as Yeung Chow fried rice. It is a popular wok fried rice dish throughout China and Chinese restaurants internationally. Depending on where you are, the ingredients may differ. Some of the staple ingredients, include cooked shrimp, cooked rice (not freshly cooked since that becomes sticky), diced cha shao pork, fresh vegetables such as peas, carrots, kai-lan, bamboo shoots and corn, chopped spring onions or scallions including the green ends, sea cucumber and crab meat and eggs.

This dish is the most popular dish to come out of the city of Yangzhou in the Jiangsiu province. Yi Bingshou, a regional magistrate for the Qing dynasty from 1754 to 1815 is credited with having invented the recipe. The dish was named Yangzhou since that was the city that Yi was the magistrate of. The dish is often served alongside thousand fish soup and has two variants. The 'silver covered gold' variant is made by scrambling the eggs separately before mixing it with the rice. The 'gold covered silver' variant is made by pouring the egg over the vegetable and rice mixture and frying all of them together. As per legend, the best cooks maintain a ratio of 3:1 or 5:1 with rice grain and egg piece.

Serves 2

Ingredients:

- 1 ½ Tbsp. vegetable or peanut oil

- 1 ½ cups leftover cooked white rice
- 1 small egg
- 2 oz. shrimp, peeled, deveined, and minced
- 2 oz. diced Chinese or honey ham
- ½ cup frozen peas
- ½ scallion, sliced thinly
- Sea salt
- Freshly ground black pepper

Instructions:

1. Moisten the rice with some water and break up. Set aside.
2. Beat the egg in a bowl until foamy. Set aside.
3. Place the wok over medium high flame and add half the vegetable or peanut oil. Swirl to coat.
4. Pour in the egg and cook for 30 seconds per side. Mince, then set aside on a plate.
5. Heat half the remaining oil, then swirl to coat. Stir in the shrimp, cook for 2 minutes, or until cooked through. Transfer to a plate and set aside.
6. Add the remaining oil and stir fry the scallions until tender. Add the rice and stir fry until dry and completely loosened.
7. Stir in the diced ham, egg, and peas. Stir fry until rice is golden and peas are warmed through.

8. Add the shrimp and stir fry until mixture is completely combined.

9. Season to taste with salt and pepper. Transfer to a takeout style box or serving dish, then serve right away.

Chapter 3 - Vegan And Vegetarian Stir Fried Dishes

Some sources cite ancient traditional Chinese dishes being meatless as far back as 25 – 60 A.D. People assume that Chinese dishes require meat of some sort. However, Chinese Buddhists and Hindus are vegetarians (for the most part with a few exceptions) so there had to be a way to create a dish just as flavorful and fulfilling as a meal with meat. By adding peanuts and almonds to dishes it gives the protein that the human body requires and adds that extra bit of flavor. Many vegetarian dishes also have complex flavor profiles by combining many different spices that cook well together.

Asparagus Tips and Bamboo Shoots

Serves 2

Ingredients:

- ½ lb. asparagus
- 1/8 cup chopped bamboo shoots, drained
- ½ Tbsp. vegetable or peanut oil
- 1 small garlic clove, minced
- ¼ tsp white sesame seeds
- Sea salt

For the Sauce:

- 1 Tbsp. vegetable broth
- ½ Tbsp. soy sauce
- ¼ tsp brown sugar
- ¼ tsp sesame oil

Instructions:

1. Combine the ingredients for the sauce in a bowl. Mix well until the sugar completely dissolves. Set aside.
2. Trim off the thick woody ends of the asparagus, then chop the asparagus stalks into bite-sized pieces. Set aside.

3. Place the wok over medium high flame and add the vegetable or peanut oil. Swirl to coat.
4. Stir in the five-spice powder and stir fry for 5 seconds, or until fragrant.
5. Stir in the garlic. Stir fry until aromatic.
6. Stir in the bamboo shoots and asparagus, stir fry for 2 minutes. Pour in the sauce and simmer for 1 minute.
7. Season to taste with salt, then place over fried rice or noodles. Top with white sesame seeds and serve immediately.

Hunan-Style Eggplant with Chopped Peanuts

Serves 2 to 3

Ingredients:
- 1 Tbsp. peanut oil
- 2 small Asian eggplants, 8 oz. each
- 2 large garlic cloves, minced
- ½ Tbsp. minced fresh ginger
- 1 Tbsp. soy sauce
- ½ Tbsp. plain rice vinegar
- ¼ cup vegetable broth
- ½ Tbsp. Chinese chili paste
- 1 tsp sugar
- 2 scallions, green parts, sliced thinly
- 2 Tbsp. chopped roasted peanuts
- ¼ Tbsp. toasted sesame oil
- Sea salt
- Freshly ground black pepper

Instructions:

1. Slice the eggplants into bite-sized cubes, place in a colander and add sea salt. Toss to combine. Set aside for 30 minutes.

2. After 30 minutes, rinse the eggplants and drain thoroughly. Blot dry with paper towels.
3. Place the wok over a medium high flame and add the vegetable oil. Swirl to coat.
4. Add the eggplant and stir fry until tender. Stir in the ginger and garlic. Stir fry for 1 minute.
5. Add the broth, chili paste, vinegar, sugar and soy sauce. Stir fry until the eggplant has absorbed the mixture. Set to medium flame and stir in the scallion and roasted peanuts. Mix well.
6. Drizzle the sesame oil into the dish. Stir fry until combined.
7. Season to taste with salt and pepper, then place over fried rice or noodles and serve immediately.

Garlic Broccoli

Serves 2

Ingredients:

- ½ Tbsp. vegetable or peanut oil
- 2 ½ cups chopped broccoli florets
- 1 small garlic clove, minced
- 2 ½ Tbsp. water
- Sea salt
- Freshly ground black pepper

Instructions:

1. Place the wok over medium high flame. Add the vegetable oil. Swirl to coat.
2. Stir in the garlic and stir fry until fragrant. Add the broccoli and stir fry for 1 minute or until crisp tender.
3. Pour in the water, cover and let steam for about 2 minutes, or until the liquid evaporates.
4. Uncover and season to taste with salt and pepper. Place over fried rice or noodles and serve immediately.

Glazed Five-Spice Carrots

It's not known how the five-spice powder came to being, but it is widely speculated that the Chinese invented it whilst trying to create a 'wonder powder', one that would include all the five elements of taste – bitter, sweet, sour, salty and pungent. Others believe that a cook stumbled across the perfect combination of spices accidentally and realized how much flavor this powder could add to a dish.

The combinations of spices used in five-spice powder vary from brand to brand. Some such preparations should be called seven-spice powder since they use seven rather than five ingredients. The standard spices used are star anise, cloves, fennel, cinnamon and Szechuan peppercorns. However, other variations can include spices such as nutmeg, cassia, ginger and licorice.

Serves 2

Ingredients:

- ½ Tbsp. vegetable oil
- ½ lb. carrots, chopped thinly on the diagonal
- 1/3 tsp five-spice powder
- 1 Tbsp. soy sauce
- 1 Tbsp. dark brown sugar
- 1/3 cup water
- ¼ Tbsp. toasted sesame oil

- Sea salt
- Freshly ground black pepper

Instructions:

1. Place the wok over a medium high flame and add the vegetable oil. Swirl to coat.

2. Stir in the five-spice powder and stir fry for 5 seconds, or until fragrant.

3. Stir in the carrots, sugar, soy sauce and water, and stir fry until combined. Increase to a high flame and let boil.

4. Once boiling, reduce to a medium low heat and cover. Let simmer for 5 minutes, or until the carrots are tender.

5. Uncover and season to taste with salt and pepper. Continue to stir fry until the liquid has dried out, then stir in the sesame oil. Place over fried rice or noodles and serve right away.

Ginger-Garlic Baby Bok Choy

Bok choy or pak choi is a type of Chinese cabbage that doesn't form heads. Instead, it forms a cluster the way mustard or celery does. Originally grown in south-east Asia and southern China, today they are grown in Northern Europe too. The name means 'white vegetable' and is also spelled pak choy or bok choi.

Serves 2

Ingredients:

- 2 garlic cloves, slivered
- ½ Tbsp. chopped fresh ginger
- ¾ lb. baby bok choy, root ends trimmed
- 2 ½ Tbsp. vegetable broth
- ½ Tbsp. soy sauce
- ¼ Tbsp. cornstarch
- ¾ Tbsp. vegetable or peanut oil
- ¼ Tbsp. toasted sesame oil
- Sea salt
- Freshly ground black pepper

Instructions:

1. Combine the cornstarch and soy sauce in a bowl. Set aside.

2. Place the wok over medium high flame, add the vegetable or peanut oil. Swirl to coat.

3. Stir in the garlic and ginger. Stir fry for 5 seconds, or until fragrant.

4. Add the baby bok choy and stir fry until wilted and bright green.

5. Set to medium flame and pour in the vegetable broth. Mix well, cover and simmer for 3 minutes, or until the bok choy is tender.

6. Uncover, add the soy sauce and cornstarch mixture. Mix in the sesame oil, then stir fry until the sauce thickens.

7. Season to taste with salt and pepper, then place over fried rice or noodles. Serve immediately.

Buddha's Delight

Traditionally favored by Buddhist monks, today Buddha's Delight is a common vegetarian favorite in most Chinese restaurants worldwide. It is also called Luóhàn zhāi, lo hon jai or lo han jai. In simplified Chinese it is also known as Luóhàn cài. It contains many vegetables although eggs or seafood can be added too.

Tradition dictates that Buddha's Delight be served in Chinese households during Chinese New Year, specifically on the first day. This is because of the belief that on the first five days of the New Year, the Chinese should maintain a vegetarian diet as a means of purifying themselves. The dish contains rare ingredients such as arrowhead and fat choy; these ingredients are only used in the dish over the New Year period.

Serves 2

Ingredients:

- ½ Tbsp. vegetable or peanut oil
- ¾ tsp minced fresh ginger
- 2 oz. bean thread noodles
- ¼ cup snow peas, trimmed
- 2 ½ Tbsp. chopped bamboo shoots, drained
- 2 ½ Tbsp. chopped water chestnuts
- 4 dried lily buds

- 4 dried shiitake mushrooms
- ¼ lb. extra firm tofu
- ½ cup shredded napa cabbage

For the Sauce:
- ½ cup vegetable broth
- ¾ Tbsp. hoisin sauce
- 1 ½ Tbsp. soy sauce
- ½ Tbsp. light brown sugar
- ½ Tbsp. sesame oil

Instructions:

1. Place the lily buds and shiitake mushrooms in a bowl, add warm water. Set aside for 20 minutes to soak.
2. Place the bean thread noodles in a bowl. Add warm water to cover. Soak for 10 minutes, drain thoroughly and set aside.
3. After 20 minutes, drain the mushrooms and lily buds and press out as much excess water as possible with paper towels.
4. Trim off the mushroom stems and chop the caps thinly. Trim off the lily bud's black ends and halve the buds, pulling the strands apart. Set aside.
5. Rinse the tofu thoroughly, then blot dry with paper towels. Slice into bite-sized cubes.

6. Combine the ingredients for the sauce until the sugar has dissolved. Set aside.

7. Place the wok over a medium-high flame and add the vegetable or peanut oil. Swirl to coat.

8. Stir in the ginger, cook until fragrant, then add the lily buds, mushrooms, snow peas, bamboo shoots, cabbage, tofu and water chestnuts. Carefully stir fry to combine.

9. Pour in the sauce, increase heat and bring to a boil. Once boiling, reduce to a simmer.

10. Cover the wok and simmer for 2 minutes, then add the noodles. Cover again and simmer for 5 minutes, or until the noodles are completely cooked and the sauce thickens.

11. Transfer to a takeout style box or serving dish and serve immediately.

Ginger Veggie Stir Fry

Serves 6

Ingredients

- 1 Tbsp. cornstarch
- ¾ cup carrots, julienned
- 1 ½ cloves garlic, crushed
- ½ cup green beans
- 2 tsp chopped fresh ginger root, divide
- 2 Tbsp. soy sauce
- ¼ cup vegetable oil, divided
- 2 ½ Tbsp. water
- 1 small head of broccoli, cut into florets
- ¼ cup onions, chopped
- ½ cup snow peas
- ½ Tbsp. salt

Instructions

1. Mix cornstarch, 1 tsp ginger, garlic, and 2 Tbsp. of vegetable oil in a large bowl. Blend until the cornstarch dissolves.
2. Add broccoli, carrots, green beans and snow peas to the mix.

3. Toss the vegetables to give them a light coating of the mix.

4. Heat the remaining 2 Tbsp. of vegetable oil in a wok over medium heat.

5. Add the vegetables. Cook for 2 minutes. Keep stirring continuously so that the vegetables don't burn.

6. Stir in the soy sauce and water.

7. Add the remaining teaspoon of ginger, onions and salt.

8. Cook the vegetables until they are tender but still retain their crispness.

Chapter 4 – Stir Fried Meat Dishes

Chicken Kung Pao

Originating in Sichuan and an indelible part of the Sichuan cuisine, Kung Pao Chicken is also known as Kung Po and Gong Bao chicken. This dish is spicy and consists of chicken, vegetables, peanuts and chili peppers as the main ingredients. It is cooked throughout China, although some regions tend to make it less spicy than the original Sichuan serving.

It is believed that the dish was named after Ding Baozhen (1820-1886), who was an official in the late Qing dynasty. He was also the governor of the province of Sichuan. The title officially given to him was Gongbao; the title is where the name of the dish derives from. However, during the Cultural Revolution, the name of the dish was considered unfit in political terms because of the association with Ding. For some time, the dish was known by other names such as Hongbao Jiding, which means 'fast fried chicken cubes'. The original name was restored in the 1980s when Deng Xiaoping instituted several reforms.

Serves 2

Ingredients:

- ½ lb. boneless, skinless chicken breast, chopped into bite-sized cubes
- 1 Tbsp. vegetable or peanut oil
- 2 scallions, white and green parts, sliced thinly
- 1 garlic clove, minced
- 4 dried red chilies
- 2 Tbsp. unsalted dry roasted peanuts
- ½ tsp minced fresh ginger

For the Marinade:

- 1 tsp dry sherry or Chinese rice wine
- ½ Tbsp. soy sauce
- ¾ tsp cornstarch

For the Sauce:

- ½ Tbsp. balsamic vinegar or Chinese black vinegar
- 1 tsp sugar
- ½ tsp sesame oil
- ½ tsp hoisin sauce
- ½ tsp soy sauce
- ½ tsp cornstarch
- ¼ tsp ground Sichuan pepper

Instructions:

1. Combine all the ingredients for the marinade in a large bowl. Add the chicken and turn several times to coat. Set aside for 10 minutes.

2. Meanwhile, combine the ingredients for the sauce in a separate bowl. Set aside.

3. Place the wok over a medium high flame and add the vegetable or peanut oil. Swirl to coat.

4. Add the chilies and stir fry until fragrant. Add the chicken and stir fry until cooked through.

5. Stir in the garlic, ginger, and chopped white part of the scallions. Stir fry for 20 seconds, then add the sauce and stir fry to combine.

6. Add the peanuts. Stir fry for 1 minute.

7. Garnish with the green part of the scallions, then serve right away with hot rice or noodles.

General Tso's Chicken

This chicken dish is more popular in American Chinese cuisine, rather than traditional Chinese cuisine. It is named after Zuo Zongtang, a military leader and statesman in the Qing dynasty. There is no indication of any connection between the general and this dish, nor is there any connection with the general's home province of Hunan.

It is said that this dish was derived from a simple Hunan chicken recipe. The reference to 'Zongtang' has nothing to do with the general and instead refers to the word 'zongtang' which means ancestral meeting hall. This explanation could be backed by the fact that the dish is found in Chinese as 'Zuo ancestral hall chicken' although this is not very common.

Another story claims that the dish was invented by a Taiwan based chef called Peng Chang-kuei who specialized in Hunan cuisine and had apprenticed under a famous twentieth century Chinese chef called Cao Jingchen. Peng fled to Taiwan with the Kuomintang forces and then went on to own his own restaurant in New York. It was there that Peng started experimenting with various dishes and recipes. One of the recipes he thought up was General Tso's Chicken recipe. Peng's Restaurant in New York claims that it was the first to serve up this dish.

The same claim is made by another restaurant – Shun Lee Palaces in New York. According to them, the dish was invented by a Chinese immigrant T.T. Wang in 1972.

Some say that both claims could be true if one were to consider that the current version of the recipe in which the meat is fried crisp was an alteration introduced by Wang to the original recipe by Peng, who cooked the chicken differently.

Ingredients

- 1 lb. skinless, boneless chicken thighs cut into chunks of ½ to ¾ inches.
- 1 ½ quarts canola, peanut or vegetable oil for deep frying
- Steamed white rice

For the marinade

- 2 Tbsp. dark soy sauce
- 1 egg white
- 2 Tbsp. 80 proof vodka
- 2 Tbsp. Shaoxing wine or dry sherry
- 3 Tbsp. corn starch
- ¼ tsp baking soda

For the dry coating

- ½ cup cornstarch

- ½ cup flour
- ½ tsp kosher salt
- ½ tsp baking powder

For the sauce

- 2 Tbsp. Shaoxing wine or dry sherry
- 3 Tbsp. dark soy sauce
- 3 Tbsp. store bought or homemade low sodium chicken stock
- 2 Tbsp. distilled white vinegar or Chinese rice vinegar
- 4 Tbsp. sugar
- 1 Tbsp. cornstarch
- 1 tsp roasted sesame seed oil
- 2 tsp vegetable, canola or peanut oil
- 2 tsp fresh ginger, minced
- 2 tsp garlic, minced
- 2 tsp minced scallion bottoms
- 6 to 8 scallions, only the white parts, cut into lengths of 1 inch each
- 8 small dried red Chinese or Arbol chilies

Instructions

1. Beat the egg whites in a large bowl until they become a little foamy.

2. Add in the wine, vodka and soy sauce and whisk together.
3. In a small bowl, take out about half of the marinade.
4. In the large bowl, add cornstarch and baking soda.
5. Put the chicken in the large bowl and turn it using your fingers so that it is coated evenly on all sides.
6. Cover the chicken with plastic wrap and put to one side.
7. In another large bowl, take baking powder, cornstarch, ½ teaspoon salt and flour and mix it.
8. Add the remainder of the marinade and mix it until the mix has coarse mealy looking clumps.
9. In another small bowl, take vinegar, wine, chicken stock, soy sauce, cornstarch, sesame seed oil and sugar and mix until there are no lumps.
10. Heat up a wok and add oil.
11. In the wok, add minced scallions, ginger, garlic and red chilies. Cook on medium heat until the vegetables have turned soft and become aromatic but aren't brown.
12. Heat the 1 ½ quarts of oil in a large wok.
13. Add the chicken to the dry coat mixture. Make sure the chicken is coated evenly before adding another piece. Once all the pieces are added, toss the chicken using your hands until all the chicken is completely coated.

14. Put the chicken, one piece at a time, into the oil. Once all the chicken is in, stir it with a pair of chopsticks.

15. Cook the chicken until it is crispy and well-cooked.

16. Take it out and place onto paper towels so that the oil can drain.

17. Add the chicken to the skillet or wok that the sauce was in. Add the sauce back in and use a spatula to turn the chicken so that all the pieces have a good coating of sauce. Serve with steamed white rice.

Sesame Chicken

Serves 4 to 6

Ingredients

- 1 lb. skinless, boneless chicken thighs cut into chunks of ½ to ¾ inches.
- 1 ½ quarts canola, peanut or vegetable oil for deep frying
- Steamed white rice and steamed broccoli

For the marinade

- 2 Tbsp. dark soy sauce
- 1 egg white
- 2 Tbsp. 80 proof vodka
- 2 Tbsp. Shaoxing wine or dry sherry
- 3 Tbsp. corn starch
- ¼ tsp baking soda

For the dry coating

- ½ cup cornstarch
- ½ cup flour
- ½ tsp kosher salt
- ½ tsp baking powder

For the sauce

- 2 Tbsp. Shaoxing wine or dry sherry
- 3 Tbsp. dark soy sauce
- 3 Tbsp. store bought or homemade low sodium chicken stock
- 2 Tbsp. distilled white vinegar or Chinese rice vinegar
- 5 Tbsp. sugar
- 1 Tbsp. cornstarch
- 2 tsp roasted sesame seed oil
- 2 tsp vegetable, canola or peanut oil
- 2 tsp fresh ginger, minced
- 2 tsp garlic, minced
- 2 tsp minced scallion bottoms
- 2 Tbsp. toasted sesame seeds

Instructions

1. Beat the egg whites in a large bowl until they become a little foamy.
2. Add in the wine, vodka and soy sauce and whisk together.
3. In a small bowl, take out about half of the marinade.
4. In the large bowl, add cornstarch and baking soda.
5. Put the chicken in the large bowl and turn it using your fingers so that it is coated properly on all sides.

6. Cover the chicken with a plastic wrap and keep it aside.
7. In another large bowl, take baking powder, cornstarch, ½ teaspoon salt and flour and mix it.
8. Add the remainder of the marinade and mix it till the mix has coarse mealy looking clumps.
9. In another small bowl, take vinegar, wine, chicken stock, soy sauce, cornstarch, sesame seed oil and sugar and mix till there are no lumps.
10. Heat up a wok and add oil.
11. In the wok add minced scallions, ginger, garlic and red chilies and cook on medium flame till the vegetables have turned soft and become aromatic but aren't browned.
12. Stir the sauce mix and add it into the wok. Make sure that you scrape out any starch or sugar that has sunk to the bottom.
13. Cook the sauce until it boils and thickens. This should take a minute or so.
14. Add half of the sesame seeds to the sauce and then take it out of the wok. Don't wipe the wok clean.
15. Heat the 1 ½ quarts of oil in a large wok.
16. Add the chicken to the dry coat mixture. Before adding the next piece, make sure to toss the current piece of chicken so that it is thoroughly coated. When all the pieces are added, toss the chicken

using your hands so no part of the chicken remains uncoated.

17. Put the chicken, one piece at a time, into the oil. Once all the chicken is in, stir it with a pair of chopsticks.

18. Cook the chicken until it is crispy and well-cooked.

19. Take it out onto paper towels so that the oil can drain.

20. Put the chicken in the skillet or wok that the sauce was in. Add the sauce in and use a spatula to turn the chicken so that all pieces have a good coating of sauce. Sprinkle the remainder of the sesame seeds on the chicken pieces. Serve with steamed white rice and steamed broccoli.

Beef with Broccoli Stir Fry

Serves 3

Ingredients

- 300 grams' lean beef
- 350 grams' broccoli
- 2 cloves garlic, sliced
- 1 tsp ginger, finely chopped

For the marinade

- ½ Tbsp. corn flour or potato starch
- ½ egg white
- 1 Tbsp. light soy sauce
- ½ Tbsp. shaoxing wine or rice wine
- 1 Tbsp. oyster sauce
- ½ Tbsp. demerara sugar
- ½ tsp ground black pepper

For the seasoning

- Salt to taste
- 1 tsp corn flour or potato starch mixed with 2 Tbsp. water

Instructions

1. Slice or julienne the beef as per your preference.

2. Add the ingredients of the marinade to the beef and marinade for 30 minutes.
3. If you want the beef to be a bit softer and have more texture, add ¼ tsp of bicarbonate soda. You can also use Eggs for this.
4. Cut the broccoli into small florets.
5. Boil some water with one or two teaspoons of salt mixed in.
6. Blanch the broccoli for twenty to thirty seconds.
7. Drain the water.
8. Immediately put the broccoli in cold or iced water to cool it.
9. Heat a wok. Add the oil. Wait for the oil to heat.
10. Add the ginger and garlic and stir fry until aromatic.
11. Add the marinated beef. Stir fry for a minute.
12. Remove the beef and set it aside.
13. Wash the wok and then dry it.
14. Again, heat up some oil and add the broccoli.
15. Stir fry for about twenty seconds.
16. Add in the beef and stir fry for thirty seconds more.
17. Add in the corn flour or potato starch mix and cook for another twenty seconds.
18. Add salt as per your taste and serve with hot white rice.

Pork Or Beef Chop Suey

Serves 4 to 6

Ingredients

- 1 lb. beef or pork (no pork chops – they are too dry)
- 2 small bunches of bok choy or broccoli, based on your preference
- ½ lb. fresh mushrooms, washed and dried with a paper towel
- ½ cup bamboo shoots, rinsed
- 1 large green pepper
- ½ cup water chestnuts, fresh
- 1 onion
- 2 stalks of celery
- ½ lb. snow peas (if you like them)
- Oil for stir frying

For the marinade

- 1-2 tsp oyster sauce
- 1 tsp soy sauce
- ½ to 1 tsp cornstarch
- 1 tsp salt
- Pepper to taste

For the sauce

- 2 tsp oyster sauce
- 4 Tbsp. water or chicken broth
- ¾ to 1 tsp cornstarch

Instructions

1. Cut the meat into thin strips.
2. Add the marinade to the meat, adding the cornstarch in at the end.
3. Marinade the meat for ten to fifteen minutes.
4. Make the sauce by whisking together all the ingredients. Do this while the pork is marinating.
5. Cut the bamboo shoots into thin strips.
6. Slice the water chestnuts and mushrooms.
7. Cut up the green pepper, remove all the seeds and slice into diagonally strips.
8. Separate each stalk and leaf of the bok choy.
9. Cut the leaves and stalk diagonally.
10. Cut the celery stalks diagonally.
11. Slice the onion into thin strips.
12. Keep all the vegetables separate on a large tray.
13. Heat up a wok and add oil.
14. Once the oil is heated up, add the meat.
15. Stir fry until the meat is brown with no pink bits.

16. Remove the meat and set it aside.

17. Heat the wok up again and add some more oil for stir frying.

18. Stir fry each vegetable separately. While stir frying the bok choy, put the stalks in first. Make sure you add salt to each vegetable while stir frying it. To cook the bok choy, add some water and then cover the wok, since the bok choy is a fairly dry vegetable.

19. Once again, heat up the wok and add more oil.

20. Add in the meat and vegetables together.

21. Push the meat and the vegetables up the sides so that a well is formed in the center.

22. Stir the sauce and add it to the well in the center of the pan.

23. Keep stirring the sauce until it thickens.

24. Once the sauce has boiled, remove the chop suey from the wok and serve it while it is hot.

Easy Orange Chicken Stir Fry

Ingredients

- 4 skinless, boneless chicken breasts halves, cut into 1 inch cubes

For the marinade

- 1 Tbsp. cornstarch
- 2 Tbsp. Chinese rice wine or dry sherry

For the sauce

- 2 Tbsp. dark soy sauce
- 1/3 cup orange juice
- 1 tsp brown sugar
- 1 tsp sesame oil
- 1 slice ginger, minced
- 1 clove garlic, minced
- ¼ tsp Chili paste
- Oil as needed for stir frying

Instructions

1. Put the chicken in a bowl and add the marinade ingredients.
2. Allow the chicken to marinade for 30 minutes.
3. Prepare the ingredients for the sauce and the garlic and ginger while the chicken is marinating.

4. Heat the wok.
5. Once the wok is hot, add the oil.
6. Once the oil is heated enough, add in the ginger and garlic.
7. Stir fry until they are aromatic.
8. Add the chicken.
9. Stir fry the chicken until the color changes.
10. Push the chicken up the sides of the wok to form a well in the middle of the wok.
11. Add the sauce to the well.
12. Combine the sauce and the chicken.
13. Stir fry for another minute and then serve.

Lettuce Wraps

Serves 6

Ingredients

- 1 head of romaine lettuce or iceberg lettuce leaves
- 1 garlic clove, minced
- 1 slice ginger, minced
- 1 Tbsp. Asian sesame oil
- 1 lb. sliced white chicken meat or meat from chicken breasts
- 2 chopped green onions
- 1 can water chestnuts, rinsed in warm running water and chopped
- 1 seeded and diced red pepper
- 1 diced stalk of celery
- 1 tsp cornstarch mixed with 2 Tbsp. of water

For the sauce

- 2 Tbsp. oyster sauce
- 1 Tbsp. soy sauce
- 1 tsp sugar
- 1 Tbsp. dry sherry

Instructions

1. Wash the lettuce.
2. Dry it and separate the leaves. Leave to one side.
3. Mix the ingredients for the sauce together.
4. Heat the sesame oil in a wok or nonstick frying pan on a high heat.
5. Add the green onions, ginger and garlic.
6. Fry until the ginger and garlic are aromatic.
7. Add the chicken.
8. Cook the chicken until it is browned.
9. Remove the chicken from the pan and set it aside.
10. Add the water chestnuts, celery and red pepper to the wok or frying pan.
11. Add the ingredients for the sauce and cook them on a medium heat.
12. Stir the cornstarch and water mix. Add it to the sauce.
13. Stir until the sauce thickens.
14. Add the chicken to the wok.
15. Cook for another two to three minutes, while stirring, until the chicken is cooked.
16. Spread out a lettuce leaf.
17. Add a heaped teaspoon of the chicken and vegetable sauce mix into the middle of the leaf.

18. Do this with all the leaves and serve.

Moo Goo Gai Pan

Serves 2

Ingredients:

- 1 Tbsp. vegetable or peanut oil
- 1/3 lb. boneless, skinless chicken breasts, sliced into thin strips
- ¼ lb. white button or cremini mushroom caps, quartered
- 2 oz. snow peas, halved
- ½ tsp minced fresh ginger
- ½ tsp minced garlic
- Sea salt
- Freshly ground black pepper

For the Marinade:

- ¾ Tbsp. dry sherry or Chinese rice wine
- ¾ Tbsp. soy sauce
- ½ tsp cornstarch

For the Sauce:

- 2 Tbsp. chicken broth
- 1 tsp oyster sauce
- 1 tsp soy sauce
- ½ Tbsp. dry sherry or Chinese rice wine

- ½ tsp cornstarch
- ½ tsp sugar

Instructions:

1. Combine the ingredients for the marinade in a large bowl. Add the chicken and turn several times to coat. Set aside for 10 minutes.
2. Meanwhile, combine all ingredients for the sauce in a separate bowl and set aside.
3. Place the wok over medium to high flame and add the vegetable or peanut oil. Swirl to coat.
4. Place the chicken and marinade into the wok and stir fry until cooked through. Transfer to a plate and set aside.
5. Stir the ginger and garlic into the wok until fragrant, then stir in the mushrooms and snow peas. Stir fry until tender.
6. Add the chicken and sauce, then stir fry until the sauce thickens. Season to taste with salt and pepper.
7. Serve straight away on a bed of hot rice or noodles.

Mongolian Beef

Serves 2

Ingredients:

- 1/2 Tbsp. vegetable or peanut oil
- ½ lb. flank steak, sliced against the grain into thin strips
- 1 leek, white part, sliced thinly
- ½ scallion, chopped
- ½ tsp minced fresh ginger

For the Marinade:

- ½ Tbsp. dry sherry or Chinese rice wine
- ½ Tbsp. soy sauce
- 1 tsp cornstarch

For the Sauce:

- 1 Tbsp. soy sauce
- 1 tsp dry sherry or Chinese rice wine
- 1 tsp chili sauce
- 1 tsp hoisin sauce
- ½ tsp sesame oil
- ½ tsp oyster sauce
- ¼ tsp crushed red pepper flakes

Instructions:

1. Combine all the ingredients for the marinade in a large bowl. Add the beef and turn several times to coat. Set aside for 10 minutes.
2. Meanwhile, combine all the ingredients for the sauce in a separate bowl and set aside.
3. Place the wok over a medium to high flame and add the vegetable or peanut oil. Swirl to coat.
4. Pour in the beef with the marinade and let simmer, untouched, for 1 minute. Stir fry until browned all over, but not cooked through.
5. Add the ginger and leek, then stir fry until the leek wilts.
6. Add in the sauce, then stir fry until everything is thoroughly combined and beef is cooked through.
7. Garnish with scallions, then serve right away with hot rice or noodles

Sweet and Sour Pork

Serves 2

Ingredients:

- 1 cup and ½ Tbsp. vegetable or peanut oil
- ½ lb. boneless pork loin, chopped into bite-sized chunks
- ½ cup pineapple chunks, canned or fresh
- ½ Tbsp. minced garlic
- ½ tsp minced fresh ginger

For the Batter:

- 1 large egg
- 2 Tbsp. all-purpose flour
- 2 Tbsp. cornstarch

For the Sauce:

- 1 ½ Tbsp. water
- 1 Tbsp. fresh or canned pineapple juice or orange juice
- 1 Tbsp. ketchup
- ¾ Tbsp. cider vinegar
- 1 Tbsp. sugar
- ½ Tbsp. soy sauce

- ½ Tbsp. Worcestershire sauce

Instructions:

1. Beat the egg in a bowl, then mix in the flour and cornstarch. Add the chopped pork and toss to coat. Set aside for 10 minutes.
2. Meanwhile, combine all the ingredients for the sauce in a separate bowl and set aside.
3. Pour 1 cup of vegetable or peanut oil into a wok and heat to 350 degrees F. Add the pork cubes and fry until golden brown all over. Work in batches, if necessary.
4. Transfer the pork to a plate lined with paper towels and blot excess oil. Set aside.
5. Drain the oil and wipe the wok clean with a paper towel. Add the remaining oil and heat over a medium to high flame.
6. Stir in the ginger and garlic for 8 seconds, then immediately add the pineapple and sauce. Toss to coat.
7. Simmer the sauce for 2 minutes, or until the pineapple is tender. Add the pork and stir fry until combined.
8. Serve right away with hot rice or noodles.

Chapter 5 – Stir Fried Seafood Dishes

Garlic Pepper Crabs

Serves 2

Ingredients:

- 1 ½ Tbsp. vegetable oil
- 1 ½ lb. fresh medium crabs
- ¼ cup chicken broth
- ½ Tbsp. minced garlic
- ¼ tsp sugar
- ¼ tsp sea salt
- ½ Tbsp. freshly ground black pepper
- 1 scallion, chopped

Instructions:

1. Clean and scrub the crabs, then chop the claws from the crabs. Discard the carapace and scrape out the gills and roe. Rinse and halve. Break the claws.
2. Place the wok over a medium to high flame and add half the vegetable oil. Swirl to coat.
3. Stir fry the black pepper with the garlic until fragrant, then add the crab pieces and stir fry for 3 minutes.

4. Sprinkle the salt and sugar over everything, then toss to combine. Pour in the chicken broth, then cover and simmer for 5 minutes or until the broth evaporates.

5. Uncover, add the scallions, and transfer to a serving plate and serve right away with hot rice or noodles.

Shrimp With Lobster Sauce

Serves 3 to 4

Ingredients

- ¾ lb. frozen tiger shrimp
- ¼ tsp salt
- 1 Tbsp. dry sherry or Chinese rice wine
- 1 tsp cornstarch
- 1 chopped green onion
- 2 tsp minced ginger
- 3 Tbsp. oil for stir frying

For the sauce

- 1/4 lb. ground pork
- 1 tsp cornstarch
- Pepper to taste
- 2 tsp soy sauce
- 1 clove of garlic
- 1 Tbsp. fermented black beans
- 1 Tbsp. soy sauce
- 2 green onions also known as scallops or spring onions
- 1 Tbsp. sherry

- ¾ cup chicken broth
- 1 tsp granulated sugar
- 1 Tbsp. cornstarch
- 2 beaten eggs
- 2 Tbsp. water
- 2 Tbsp. oil for stir frying
- ¼ tsp salt

Instructions

For the sauce

1. Add the soy sauce, 1 teaspoon cornstarch and pepper to the pork and allow it to marinate for fifteen minutes.
2. Let the black beans sit in water for a few minutes so that they soften up and then rinse them.
3. Drain them and use a knife or cleaver to chop them up finely.
4. Peel the garlic clove and mince it.
5. Mash the black beans and the clove of garlic together.
6. Wash the green onion and cut it diagonally into pieces of 1 inch.
7. Take a small bowl and mix the chicken broth, sherry, sugar and soy sauce together.

8. In another small bowl, mix the cornstarch in the water and stir.
9. Beat the eggs lightly after adding salt to them.
10. Heat up the wok on a high flame.
11. Add 2 tablespoons of oil and swirl the wok so that the oil coats the sides.
12. Add half of the mashed garlic and black beans to the oil.
13. Stir fry the mix until it is aromatic.
14. Add the ground pork and stir fry until the color of the pork changes.
15. Remove everything from the wok and clean it.
16. Reheat the wok and add 1 tablespoon of oil.
17. Once the oil is hot, add the rest of the garlic and black bean mash.
18. Stir fry until it is aromatic.
19. Add the sauce of chicken broth, sherry, sugar and soy sauce.
20. Stir the cornstarch and water mix again and add it to the wok.
21. Add the ground pork along with the green onions.
22. Stir in the eggs just before serving the sauce.

For the shrimp

1. Keep the lobster sauce warm.

2. Run the shrimp under running water until it has thawed.
3. Pat the shrimp dry using paper towels.
4. Marinate the shrimp in the sherry or rice wine, cornstarch and salt for about fifteen minutes.
5. Heat the wok over a high flame.
6. Add the oil.
7. Once the oil is hot, add the green onion and ginger.
8. Stir fry until the ginger and green onion are aromatic.
9. Add the shrimp and stir fry until the color of the shrimp changes to pink.
10. Push the shrimp up the walls of the wok to create a well in the middle.
11. Add the lobster sauce into the well.
12. Let the sauce come to a boil and then mix the shrimp with it. Serve it while it is hot.

Chili Shrimp

Serves 2

Ingredients:

- ½ lb. large shrimp, peeled and deveined
- 1 ½ Tbsp. vegetable oil
- 1 Tbsp. dry sherry or Chinese rice wine
- 1 Tbsp. chopped scallions
- 1 Tbsp. minced ginger
- ½ Tbsp. minced fresh chilies
- ½ Tbsp. sea salt

For the Sauce:

- 1 Tbsp. soy sauce
- ½ tsp chili bean sauce
- ¼ tsp sugar

Instructions:

1. Stir the salt into a bowl filled with 1 ½ cups of cold water. Place the shrimp in the brine and set aside for an hour.
2. After an hour, drain the shrimp and blot dry with paper towels. Set aside to dry completely.
3. Meanwhile, combine the chili bean sauce, soy sauce, and sugar in a bowl.

4. Place the wok over a medium to high flame and add half of the vegetable oil. Swirl to coat.

5. Place the shrimp into the wok and stir fry until pink. Add the rice wine and swirl, then immediately transfer to a plate and set aside.

6. In the remaining oil in the wok, stir fry the scallions, chilies and ginger until fragrant.

7. Add the sauce and shrimp, then stir fry until shrimp is cooked through and coated in the sauce. Serve right away with hot rice or noodles.

Fish Steaks in Black Bean Sauce

Serves 2

Ingredients:

- 1 ½ Tbsp. vegetable oil
- ¾ lb. boneless tuna, snapper, sea bass, or halibut steaks, sliced into bite-sized chunks
- 2 garlic cloves, minced
- 1 Tbsp. black bean paste
- ½ tsp sugar
- ½ tsp freshly ground black pepper
- 3 scallions, chopped

For the Marinade:

- 1 ½ Tbsp. minced fresh ginger
- 1 Tbsp. dry sherry or Chinese rice wine
- ½ tsp sesame oil

Instructions:

1. Combine all the ingredients for the marinade in a large bowl. Add the fish and turn several times to coat. Set aside for 30 minutes.
2. Place the wok over a medium to high flame and add half the vegetable oil. Swirl to coat.

3. Add the garlic and fish with marinade. Stir fry until fish is opaque.

4. Stir in the black bean paste and stir fry for 2 minutes.

5. Add the black pepper, sugar and scallion. Stir fry until fish is cooked through.

6. Serve right away with hot rice or noodles.

Conclusion

I hope this book helped you to learn how to cook simple, tasty and easy stir fry Chinese dishes.

The next step is to gather your ingredients and tools and start cooking. These dishes taste best when served immediately, but any leftovers also hold up wonderfully if stored and reheated properly. Never again will you have to order possibly unhealthy take-outs when you can take charge of your own meals.

www.ingramcontent.com/pod-product-compliance
Lightning Source LLC
Chambersburg PA
CBHW071447070526
44578CB00001B/252